First Fridays
& First Saturdays

The Devotions Explained

*All booklets are published thanks to the
generous support of the members of the
Catholic Truth Society*

CATHOLIC TRUTH SOCIETY
PUBLISHERS TO THE HOLY SEE

Contents

*All rights reserved. Published 2008 by the Incorporated Catholic Truth
Society 40-46 Harleyford Road London, SE11 5AY Tel: 020 7640 0042
Fax: 020 7640 0046. Copyright © 2008 The Incorporated Catholic
Truth Society.*

ISBN 978 1 86082 508 8

Introduction

'Let us love and honour these two hearts which are so intimately united; let us go to God the Father through the Heart of Jesus; let us go to our Saviour through the Heart of Mary. Let us render to God the Father through the Heart of Jesus what we owe to his justice and infinite bounty, and render to God the Son, through the Heart of Mary what we owe to his clemency and his benefits in our regard. We shall obtain everything from the Father and the Holy Spirit through the Heart of Jesus and everything from the Son through the Heart of Mary.'

(From the *Manual of Prayers*, Brothers of the Christian Schools, 1952)

'Devotions' are popular prayers which are not part of the Church's official liturgy but which flow from the liturgy and in their turn help us to participate in it more fully. The Church encourages these devotions, and in the year 2001 published a document entitled *The Directory on Popular Piety and the Liturgy*, to foster these popular customs and ensure that they conform to the authentic spirit of the Gospel.

Of all the devotions familiar to Catholics, few are so deep-rooted, or have nourished so many souls, as the devotions to the Sacred Heart of Jesus and the Immaculate Heart of Mary, expressed in the observance of the First Fridays and First Saturdays. The devotion to the Sacred Heart of Jesus, in essence, is nothing other than devotion to that love with which 'God so loved the world that he gave his only Son' (*Jn* 3:16), while in honouring the Immaculate Heart of Mary, we honour the one whom the Angel Gabriel addressed as 'full of grace', and who replied in her humility, 'Let it be done to me according to your word (*Lk* 1:28-38)' - a model for every Christian.

It is to be hoped that this little book may encourage these two devotions anew, and lead many more Christians to discover the riches that can be found there.

The devotion of the First Fridays in honour of the Sacred Heart of Jesus

'This heart is still the same, always burning with love for men, always open so as to shower down graces and blessings upon us, always touched by our sorrows, always eager to impart its treasures to us and to give himself to us, always ready to receive us, to be our refuge, our dwelling place, and our heaven even in this world'.

(*St Claude de la Colombière*)

History of devotion to the Sacred Heart

We can almost say that devotion to the Sacred Heart is as old as Christianity itself. It is founded on one of the most important truths of our faith: that God became Man in Jesus Christ and that, having ascended to heaven, his sacred humanity remains united to the Godhead in the glory of the Holy Trinity. Therefore his Sacred Heart, the source and symbol of his love for us, may fittingly be made the object of our special reverence (The doctrine is expounded fully in the Encyclical of Pope Pius XII, *Haurietas Aquas*, of 1956).

Our Lord, in the Gospels, reveals himself as 'meek and humble of heart' (*Mt* 11:29) and calls his disciples to live in close communion with him, to imitate his teaching and learn from his way of life. In this lies the basis of our devotion - a desire to model ourselves on Jesus and to love Him in return for the love shown to us. Later, in the hour of his Passion, Jesus' side is pierced with a spear, and there flows out blood and water (*Jn* 19:34). This blood and water was interpreted by the Fathers of the Church as representing symbolically the waters of Baptism and the blood of the Eucharist - hence the sacramental life of the Church can be seen as flowing from the heart of Jesus, a source to which the faithful soul must always be returning.

These meditations of the Fathers bore fruit in the writings of many of the great mystics of the Middle Ages, who expressed in the language of poetry and prayer both the burning love of Christ for souls, and the love which we poor sinners should have for so good and generous a Saviour. Among these figures we can count St Bernard of Clairvaux (+1153), St Bonaventure (+1274), St Gertrude (+1302), St Catherine of Sienna (+1380) and many others.

Later, amidst the worldliness of the Renaissance and its pride in human learning, saints such as Philip Neri (+1595), the founder of the Oratory, called their contemporaries back to the simple love of God revealed in Christ Jesus. 'Who wills anything but Christ, knows not what he would have; who asks for anything but Christ, knows not for what he asks; who works and not for Christ, knows not what he does', wrote St Philip. This was also the spirit of the famous Bishop of Geneva, St Francis De Sales (+1622) who adopted humility, gentleness and tender loving mercy, all aspects of the Sacred Heart, as a model for His life and apostolate. Together with St Jane Frances de Chantal (+1641) St Francis founded the Order of the Visitation, and he devised for this order its characteristic emblem - the Heart of Jesus, pierced and crowned with thorns. About the same time, St John Eudes (+1680), a priest of the French Oratory, published a book entitled *The Life and Royalty of Jesus in the Christian Soul*, which ran to six editions. This work, and Eudes' passionate preaching, won a huge following, and it was he who first composed a Mass and Office of the Sacred

Heart, between 1668 and 1670. This led Pope Leo XIII to describe him as 'the author of the liturgical worship of the Sacred Hearts of Jesus and Mary'.

Finally, towards the end of the same century, it was a nun of the Visitation Order, St Margaret Mary Alacoque (+1690), who gave birth to devotion to the Sacred Heart in the form we know it now. It was also she who propagated the observance of the nine First Fridays.

The First Fridays

Between 1673 and 1675, at the Convent of the Visitation in Paray-le-Monial, France, St Margaret Mary was favoured with a series of visions of Our Lord, revealing to her his Sacred Heart which symbolised his love for mankind, and was so often rejected. He asked her to spread devotion to this Heart throughout the whole Church, as reparation for the many sins and offenses it endured. In a short time St Margaret Mary had discovered for herself the fruitfulness of this devotion. She wrote:

'I know of no exercise of devotion in the spiritual life better calculated to raise a soul in a short time to the height of sanctity, and to make it taste the true sweetness that is found in the service of God. If we knew how agreeable this devotion is to Jesus Christ, there is no one Christian, how little his love for this amiable Saviour, who would not practise it...I need nothing but God, and to lose myself in the Heart of Jesus'.

At this time, St Margaret Mary relied heavily on advice from her spiritual director, St Claude de la Colombière (+1682), a Jesuit priest then working at the royal court in London as chaplain to the Duchess of York. St Claude encouraged his spiritual daughter, and worked on his own account to foster devotion to the Sacred Heart. It is therefore interesting that England (despite being then almost entirely a Protestant country) was one of the first places where devotion to the Sacred Heart of Jesus was promoted in its modern form.

At the centre of the revelations received by St Margaret Mary are *twelve promises*, made to her by Jesus. In these, he promises that, in response to those who consecrate themselves and make reparations to His Sacred Heart:

1. He will give them all the graces necessary in their state of life.
2. He will establish peace in their homes.
3. He will comfort them in all their afflictions.
4. He will be their secure refuge during life, and above all, in death.
5. He will bestow abundant blessings upon all their undertakings.
6. Sinners will find in His Heart the source and infinite ocean of mercy.
7. Lukewarm souls shall become fervent.
8. Fervent souls shall quickly mount to high perfection.

9. He will bless every place in which an image of His Heart is exposed and honoured.

10. He will give to priests the gift of touching the most hardened hearts.

11. Those who shall promote this devotion shall have their names written in His Heart.

12. In the excessive mercy of His Heart, that His all-powerful love will grant to all those who receive Holy Communion on the First Fridays in nine consecutive months the grace of final perseverance; they shall not die in His disgrace, nor without receiving the sacraments. His divine Heart shall be their safe refuge in this last moment.

It should be obvious that the twelfth promise is by far the most important, and the one most especially associated with the custom of the 'First Fridays'.

We should note here that while the Church has approved of the orthodoxy of these revelations, and many Popes down to the present day have frequently encouraged devotion to the Sacred Heart, the Church has also insisted that these promises be understood correctly. We must realise that they contain no new doctrine not already found in Scripture and Tradition, nor must they be seen as encouragement to live anything less than a full and generous Christian life. To treat the promises in a superstitious or mechanistic way would be quite contrary to Our Lord's intentions.

Therefore, to understand the promises properly, and in the sense in which the Church intends, it is clear that:

1. Our Lord required Communion to be received on a particular day chosen by Him;

2. the nine Fridays must be consecutive;

3. they must be made in honour of His Sacred Heart, which means that those who make the nine Fridays must practice the devotion and must have a great love for our Lord;

4. Our Lord does not say that those who make the nine Fridays will be dispensed from any of their obligations or from exercising the vigilance necessary to lead a good life and overcome temptation; rather He implicitly promises abundant graces to those who make the nine Fridays to help them to carry out these obligations and persevere to the end;

5. perseverance in receiving Holy Communion for nine consecutive First Fridays helps the faithful to acquire the habit of frequent Communion, which our Lord eagerly desires; and

6. the practice of the nine Fridays is very pleasing to our Lord since He promises such great reward, and that all Catholics should endeavour to make the nine Fridays.*

---

* Source: *Enthronement of the Sacred Heart* by Rev Francis Larkin, SS.CC., St Paul Editions, 1978.

The elements of the devotion

With this understanding to guide us we can now move on to look at what the devotion of the First Fridays actually entails. Essentially, it consists of the following elements:

1. **Sacramental Confession**, as a preparation for;
2. **Holy Communion**, received on nine consecutive First Fridays;
3. Making a '**Holy Hour**' in the presence of the Blessed Sacrament.

As noted in the outline of the devotion given above, it is taken for granted that those practicing the First Fridays will also have a more general love for the Sacred Heart. This can be expressed in many ways, but would include, wherever possible, celebrating the Feast of the Sacred Heart, which occurs on the Friday after the second Sunday after Pentecost, and perhaps paying some special reverence to the Sacred Heart during the month of June, which is traditionally dedicated to this mystery.

We now offer some guidance and prayers which may help those wanting to make the devotion of the First Fridays to do so more fruitfully.

GUIDE TO A GOOD CONFESSION

While sacramental Confession is not explicitly required for those wishing to observe the First Fridays (as it is for those observing the First Saturdays), nevertheless it should be part of our devotion to the Sacred Heart, which is wounded by sin, and to whom we desire to make reparation. St Margaret Mary would certainly have assumed that those receiving Holy Communion on the First Fridays would have gone to Confession beforehand, since in her time the reception of Holy Communion when not preceded by Confession was considered unthinkable. The discipline of the Church has developed in this matter, and of course, anyone not in a state of mortal sin may always present themselves for Communion. Nevertheless, in order truly to honour the Sacred Heart, those receiving Communion on the First Fridays will certainly ensure that regular and frequent Confession is part of their spiritual lives, and will celebrate this Sacrament, preferably on the same day as Holy Communion, but at least as part of their immediate preparation.

The following may assist in making a good Confession.

Prayer before Confession

Almighty and merciful God,
you have brought me here in the name of your Son
to receive your mercy and grace in my time of need.

Open my eyes to see the evil I have done.
Touch my heart and convert me to yourself.
Where sin has separated me from you,
may your love unite me to you again:
where sin has brought weakness,
may your power heal and strengthen;
where sin has brought death,
may your Spirit raise to new life.
Give me a new heart to love you,
so that my life may reflect the image of your Son.
May the world see the glory
of Christ revealed in your Church,
and come to know that he is the one whom
you have sent, Jesus Christ, your Son, our Lord. Amen.

Examination of Conscience

Careful preparation is vital in order to make the most of this encounter with our loving heavenly Father. Find some time to be alone and quiet to reflect on your life, your relationship with God and others. An examination of conscience provides us with what we are going to say in the confessional. Without time given to such examination our confession is in danger of being incomplete. There are many ways: one is to use a gospel passage, especially one of the many healing miracles or occasions of forgiveness (eg. *Lk* 15:11-32; *Jn* 4:5-42; *Mt* 18:21-35; *Lk* 18:9-14). Imagine you are the person being healed or forgiven by Jesus. Read the scripture passage, imagine you are in the scene, and listen to the words of Jesus. He speaks to you! What do you say? Alternatively, Jesus summed up and extended the Ten Commandments by his two great commandments (*Mk* 12:28-42): Love God and your neighbour.

Mortal sin is sin whose object is a grave matter and which is also committed with full knowledge and deliberate consent (*CCC*, 1857). We must confess all mortal sins. We are not obliged to confess all venial sins. We commit venial sin when, in a less serious matter, we do not observe the standard prescribed by the moral law, or when we disobey the moral law in a grave matter, but without full knowledge or without complete consent (*CCC*, 1862). Confession of venial sins is an act of devotion. We need not be unduly anxious to confess them all, but may rather choose to focus on areas of our life that are most in need of God's grace.

The following examination of conscience can help us to measure our lives by the objective standard of Christ's teaching. We may also consider more generally how we may have failed in our lives to live fully as disciples of Christ.

Sins against God

Have I rejected my faith, refused to find out more about it?
Have I forgotten my daily prayers or said them badly?
Have I experimented with the occult or put my trust in fortune tellers or horoscopes?
Have I blasphemed against God or used bad language?

Have I shown disrespect for holy things, places or people?
Have I missed Mass on Sundays or Holydays through my own fault?
Have I let myself be distracted at Mass or distracted others?
Have I received Holy Communion in a state of mortal sin?
Have I received Holy Communion without proper reverence, care or thanksgiving?

Sins against myself and others

Have I been impatient, angry or jealous?
Have I brooded over injuries or refused to forgive?
Have I taken part in or encouraged abortion, the destruction of human embryos, euthanasia or any other means of taking human life?
Have I been verbally or physically violent to others?
Have I been racist in my thoughts, words or deeds?
Have I hurt anyone by speaking badly about them?
Have I betrayed confidences without good cause or revealed things simply to hurt others?
Have I judged others rashly?
Have I been drunk or used illegal drugs?
Have I driven dangerously or inconsiderately?
Have I spoken in an obscene way?
Have I looked at obscene pictures, films or books?
Have I been involved in any impure behaviour on my own or with someone else?
Have I been vain, proud, selfish or self-seeking?

Have I told lies to excuse myself, to hurt others or to make myself look more important?

Have I stolen anything?

Have I failed to contribute to the support of the Church in proportion to my means?

Have I been disobedient, rude or insolent to those in authority over me?

Have I been harsh, overbearing or sarcastic to those under my authority?

Have I cheated my employers or employees?

Have I misused or damaged the property of others?

Have I set my heart greedily on possessing things?

Have I given scandal or bad example?

Have I been lazy at my work, study or domestic duties?

Have I been jealous of others - of their looks, their popularity, their good work?

Have I encouraged others to do wrong in any way?

For spouses

Have I neglected to foster the warmth of my love and affection for my spouse?

Have I prolonged disagreements through resentment or failing to apologise when I have been in the wrong?

Have I mistreated my spouse verbally, emotionally or physically?

Have I used artificial means of birth control?

Have I been unfaithful to my spouse in any way?

For parents

Have I neglected to teach my children to pray?

Have I neglected the religious education of my children?

Have I failed to bring my children to Sunday Mass?

Have I argued with my spouse in front of my children?

Have I failed to exercise vigilance over what my children read, see on television or on the internet?

Have I been harsh or overbearing to my children?

Have I neglected my children's welfare in any way?

For young people

Have I been disobedient to my parents?

Have I been unhelpful at home?

Have I failed to try to understand my parents and talk with them?

Have I upset the peace of my home for selfish reasons?

Have I lost control when I have been angry?

Have I sulked or been sarcastic instead of asking for help?

Have I failed to work properly at school?

Have I treated teachers or other adults with disrespect?

Have I played unfairly at games or sports?

Have I taken part in fights?

An Act of Contrition

O my God, I am sorry and beg pardon for all my sins, and detest them above all things, because they deserve your dreadful punishments, because they have crucified my loving Saviour Jesus Christ, and, most of all, because they offend your infinite goodness; and I firmly resolve, by the help of your grace, never to offend you again, and carefully to avoid the occasions of sin.

Prayer after Confession

Father, in your love you have brought me from evil to good and from misery to happiness. Through your blessings give me the courage of perseverance. Amen.

RECEIVING HOLY COMMUNION DEVOUTLY

The frequent, and worthy, reception of Holy Communion is at the heart of the First Friday devotion, and that of the First Saturdays. This is only natural, since in receiving Holy Communion we enjoy a personal encounter with Jesus Christ, who is present in the Blessed Sacrament, Body, Blood, Soul and Divinity, and is at that moment able to give us all the graces we need to live our Christian lives.

St Claude de la Colombière, Spiritual Director to St Margaret Mary, had this to say about Holy Communion:

'Your usual intention at Communion should be that of Jesus Christ in coming to you, for it is the purest and most excellent possible: to unite yourself to the source and object of love, to strengthen yourself in the service of God and in the practice of virtue, to purify yourself by union with him who is Purity itself. You can add special intentions to these according to your needs and obligations'.

We can receive Holy Communion whenever we are in a state of grace, that is, when we are not aware of having committed any mortal sin. We should, however, always be careful to make regular Confession part of our spiritual lives, as noted above. We should also prepare for our Communion, by spending a few moments in quiet prayer before Mass, and we should also make a short prayer of thanksgiving when Mass is over.

You may find the following prayers useful. It is well to stop after every few words, to allow them to sink into the heart. Each prayer may be said several times.

Before Holy Communion

Prayer for Help

O God, help me to make a good Communion. Mary, my dearest mother, pray to Jesus for me. My dear Angel Guardian, lead me to the Altar of God.

Act of Faith

O God, because you have said it, I believe that I shall receive the Sacred Body of Jesus Christ to eat, and his Precious Blood to drink. My God, I believe this with all my heart.

Act of Humility

My God, I confess that I am a poor sinner; I am not worthy to receive the Body and Blood of Jesus, on account of my sins. Lord, I am not worthy to receive you under my roof; but only say the word, and my soul will be healed.

Act of Sorrow

My God, I detest all the sins of my life. I am sorry for them, because they have offended you, my God, you who are so good. I resolve never to commit sin any more. My good God, pity me, have mercy on me, forgive me.

Act of Adoration

O Jesus, great God, present on the Altar, I bow down before you. I adore you.

Act of Love and Desire

Jesus, I love you. I desire with all my heart to receive you. Jesus, come into my poor soul, and give me your Flesh to eat and your Blood to drink. Give me your whole Self, Body, Blood, Soul and Divinity, that I may live for ever with you.

Prayer of St Thomas Aquinas

Almighty and ever-living God, I approach the sacrament of your only-begotten Son, our Lord Jesus Christ. I come sick to the doctor of life, unclean to the fountain of mercy, blind to the radiance of eternal light, poor and needy to the Lord of heaven and earth. Lord in your great generosity, heal my sickness, wash away my defilement, enlighten my blindness, enrich my poverty, and clothe my nakedness. May I receive the bread of angels, the King of kings and Lord of lords, with humble reverence, with purity and faith, with repentance and love and the determined purpose that will help to bring me to salvation. May I receive the sacrament of the Lord's body and blood and its reality and power. Kind God, may I receive the body of your only begotten Son, our Lord Jesus Christ, born from the womb of the Virgin Mary, and so be received into his mystical body and numbered among his members. Loving Father, as on my earthly pilgrimage I now receive your beloved Son under the veil of a sacrament, may I one day see him face to face in glory, who lives and reigns with you for ever. Amen.

After Holy Communion

I give you thanks

I give you thanks, Lord, Holy Father, everlasting God. In your great mercy, and not because of my own merits, you have fed me a sinner and your unworthy servant, with the precious body and blood of your Son, our Lord Jesus Christ. I pray that this Holy Communion may not serve as my judgement and condemnation, but as my forgiveness and salvation. May it be my armour of faith and shield of good purpose, root out in me all that is evil and increase every virtue. I beseech you to bring me a sinner, to that great feast where, with your Son and the Holy Spirit you are the true light of your holy ones, their flawless blessedness, everlasting joy and perfect happiness. Through Christ our Lord. Amen. (St Thomas Aquinas)

Act of Faith

O Jesus, I believe that I have received your Flesh to eat and your Blood to drink, because you have said it, and your word is true. All that I have and all that I am are your gift and now you have given me yourself.

Act of Adoration

O Jesus, my God, my Creator, I adore you, because from your hands I came and with you I am to be happy for ever.

Act of Humility

O Jesus, I am not worthy to receive you, and yet you have come to me that my poor heart may learn of you to be meek and humble.

Act of Love

Jesus, I love you; I love you with all my heart. You know that I love you, and wish to love you daily more and more.

Act of Thanksgiving

My good Jesus, I thank you with all my heart. How good, how kind you are to me. Blessed be Jesus in the most holy Sacrament of the Altar.

Act of Offering

O Jesus, receive my poor offering.
Jesus, you have given yourself to me,
and now let me give myself to you:
I give you my body, that I may be chaste and pure.
I give you my soul, that I may be free from sin.
I give you my heart, that I may always love you.
I give you my every breath that I shall breathe,
and especially my last.
I give you myself in life and in death,
that I may be yours for ever and ever.

For Yourself

O Jesus, wash away my sins with your Precious Blood.
O Jesus, the struggle against temptation is not yet finished. My Jesus, when temptation comes near me, make me strong against it. In the moment of temptation may I always say: "My Jesus, mercy! Mary, help!"
O Jesus, may I lead a good life; may I die a happy death. May I receive you before I die. May I say when I am dying: "Jesus, Mary and Joseph, I give you my heart and my soul".

Listen now for a moment to Jesus Christ; perhaps he has something to say to you. Answer Jesus in your heart, and tell him all your troubles. Then say:

For Perseverance

Jesus, I am going away for a time, but I trust not without you. You are with me by your grace. I resolve never to leave you by mortal sin. Although I am so weak I have such hope in you. Give me grace to persevere. Amen.

MAKING A HOLY HOUR

As part of the devotion of the First Fridays, it is also asked that we should make a 'Holy Hour' in honour of the Sacred Heart. This is an hour of prayer spent in the presence of the Blessed Sacrament, which should be made on the Thursday preceding the First Friday. Our Lord asked St Margaret Mary to observe this Holy Hour in order to make reparation for the desolation and loneliness he felt when he prayed all alone in the garden of Gethsemane on the eve of his Passion, with no one to comfort him.

No special prayers are laid down for this Holy Hour, but the following are all very appropriate, and may be found useful (*you could also use some of the prayers given above*).

Litany of the Sacred Heart

Lord, have Mercy; *Lord, have Mercy*
Christ, have Mercy; *Christ, have Mercy*
Lord, have Mercy; *Lord, have Mercy*
God the Father in Heaven, *have Mercy on us*
(Repeat this response after each invocation)
God the Son, Redeemer of the world,
God the Holy Spirit,
Holy Trinity, one God,
Heart of Jesus, Son of the Eternal Father,
Heart of Jesus, Formed in the womb of the Virgin Mother,
Heart of Jesus, One with the Eternal Word,
Heart of Jesus, Infinite in Majesty,
Heart of Jesus, Holy Temple of God,
Heart of Jesus, Tabernacle of the Most High,
Heart of Jesus, House of God and Gate of Heaven,
Heart of Jesus, Aflame with love for us,
Heart of Jesus, Source of Justice and Love,
Heart of Jesus, Full of Goodness and Love,
Heart of Jesus, Wellspring of all Virtue,
Heart of Jesus, Worthy of all praise,
Heart of Jesus, King and Centre of all hearts,
Heart of Jesus, Treasure-house of Wisdom and Knowledge,
Heart of Jesus, In Whom dwells the fullness of God,
Heart of Jesus, In whom the Father is well-pleased,
Heart of Jesus, From Whose fullness we have all received,
Heart of Jesus, Desire of the Eternal Hills,

Heart of Jesus, Patient and full of Mercy,
Heart of Jesus, Generous to all who turn to You,
Heart of Jesus, Fountain of Life and Holiness,
Heart of Jesus, Atonement for our sins,
Heart of Jesus, Obedient even to death,
Heart of Jesus, Pierced by a lance,
Heart of Jesus, Source of all Consolation,
Heart of Jesus, Our Life and Resurrection,
Heart of Jesus, Our Peace and Reconciliation,
Heart of Jesus, Victim for our sins,
Heart of Jesus, Salvation of all who trust in You,
Heart of Jesus, Hope of all who die in You,
Heart of Jesus, Delight of all the Saints,
Lamb of God; You take away the sins of the world,
have Mercy on us.
Lamb of God, You take away the sins of the world,
have Mercy on us.
Lamb of God, You take away the sins of the world,
have Mercy on us.
V. Jesus, meek and humble of heart.
R. *Touch our hearts and make them like Your Own.*

Let us pray:
Father, we rejoice in the gifts of love we have received
from the Heart of Jesus, Your Son. Open our hearts to
share His Life and continue to bless us with His Love.
We ask this in the Name of Jesus the Lord. Amen.

Acts of Consecration

Act of Consecration
(St Claude de la Colombière)

O adorable Saviour, vouchsafe my desire to consecrate myself entirely to the love and reparation of thy divine Heart and to accept the gift I make to thee of all that I am and all that I have. In reparation for all the outrages committed against thee and for the terrible ingratitude thou dost suffer from men, I consecrate to thee myself and my life. Give and take what thou wilt; use me or set me aside as a useless instrument; give me consolations or give me trials; may thy will be done in all things. May all this glorify thy divine Heart and make reparation to it. I wish to make a full gift of all this to thee, begging thee to accept it and use it freely for the salvation of sinners. Amen.

Personal or Individual Consecration

O most Holy Heart of Jesus, fountain of every blessing, I adore You, I love You, and with a lively sorrow for my sins, I offer You this poor heart of mine. Make me humble, patient, pure and completely obedient to your Will. Grant, good Jesus, that I may live in You and for You. Protect me in the midst of danger, comfort me in all afflictions, give me health of mind, body and soul, assistance in my temporal needs, Your Blessings on all that I do, and the Grace of a holy death. Amen.

Act of Consecration

O Sacred Heart of Jesus, filled with infinite love, broken by my ingratitude, pierced by my sin, yet loving me still, accept the consecration that I make to you of all that I have and all that I am. Take every faculty of my soul and body and draw me day by day nearer and nearer to your Sacred side and there, as I may bear the lesson, teach me your blessed ways. Amen.

Consecration of Society to the Sacred Heart
(Blessed John XXIII)

O Jesus, come back into our society, our family life, our souls, and reign there as our Peaceful Sovereign. Enlighten with the splendour of faith and the charity of Your tender Heart the souls of those who work for the good of the people, for Your poor; impart to them Your Own Spirit, a spirit of discipline, order, and gentleness, preserving the flame of enthusiasm ever alight in our hearts. Amen. (From the *Story of a Soul*).

Lord Jesus, Whose Heart was once pierced for love of us, we renew our baptismal promises to reject Satan and all his works and all his empty promises to live only for You. Although we are already united to You through the Sacrament of Baptism, and this union is constantly perfected by the Eucharist, we give ourselves to You again today to fix more deeply in our hearts this resolve

to live for You and to serve You more faithfully. Give us the grace to love and serve You always. Amen.
(*Apostleship of Prayer*).

Consecration of the human race to the Sacred Heart

O most sweet Jesus, Redeemer of mankind, behold us humbly prostrate before your altar. We are yours, and yours we wish to be; and so that we may be united to you more closely, we consecrate ourselves to your most Sacred Heart. There are many who have never known you and many who have despised your teaching and rejected you. Have pity on them all most merciful Jesus and draw them to you Sacred heart. Be King not only of the faithful who have never left you, but also of the prodigal children who have abandoned you. Let them return quickly to their Father's house lest they perish from misery and deprivation. Be King of those who have been misled by error or are divided from us by schism, and call them back to the haven of truth and unity of faith, that soon there may be one fold and one Shepherd. Grant to your Church, O Lord, safety and sure liberty; grant to all nations the peace that comes from order; and may all the earth resound from pole to pole with the one chant: Praise, honour and glory be forever to the Divine Heart which accomplished our salvation. Amen.

Acts of Reparation

Reparation to the Mystical Body

Lord Jesus Christ, we look at the Cross, and we, Your Pilgrim Church, can see what sin has done to the Son of Mary, to the Son of God. But now You are Risen and Glorified. You suffer no more in the flesh. Sin can no longer expose You to the Agony in the Garden, to the scourging, to the death on a cross. But it can reach You through Your Mystical Body. This is part of You. Your Church on Earth still feels the strength of sin. For this we make our Act of Reparation.

We, who have sinned in the past, now consecrate ourselves to the healing of Your Mystical Body. Sanctify us for this task.

May Your Sacred Heart be the symbol, not of one loved, but of two. Your love for us and our love for You. Accept our love and help us make it real by serving You in all our brothers and sister, so that love and concern may lead all people to know the one true God and Jesus Christ whom He has sent. Amen.

Act of Reparation to the Most Sacred Heart of Jesus

Most sweet Jesus, whose overflowing charity for men is requited by so much forgetfulness, negligence and contempt, behold us prostrate before you, eager to repair by a special act of homage the cruel indifference and injuries to which your loving Heart is every where subject.

Mindful, alas! that we ourselves have had a share in such great indignities, which we now deplore from the depths of our hearts, we humbly ask your pardon and declare our readiness to at one by voluntary expiation, not only for our own personal offenses, but also for the sins of those, who, straying far from the path of salvation, refuse in their obstinate infidelity to follow you, their Shepherd and Leader, or, renouncing the promises of their baptism, have cast off the sweet yoke of your law.

We are now resolved to expiate each and every deplorable outrage committed against you; we are now determined to make amends for the manifold offenses against Christian modesty in unbecoming dress and behaviour, for all the foul seductions laid to ensnare the feet of the innocent, for the frequent violations of Sundays and holydays, and the shocking blasphemies uttered against you and your Saints. We wish also to make amends for the insults to which your Vicar on earth and your priests are subjected, for the profanation, by conscious neglect or terrible acts of sacrilege, of the very Sacrament of your divine love, and lastly for the public crimes of nations who resist the rights and teaching authority of the Church which you have founded.

Would that we were able to wash away such abominations with our blood. We now offer, in reparation for these violations of your divine honour, the satisfaction you once made to your Eternal Father on the cross and which you continue to renew daily on our altars; we offer it in union with the acts of atonement of your Virgin Mother and all the Saints and of the pious faithful on earth; and we sincerely promise to make recompense, as far as we can with the help of your grace, for all neglect of your great love and for the sins we and others have committed in the past. Henceforth, we will live a life of unswerving faith, of purity of conduct, of perfect observance of the precepts of the Gospel and especially that of charity. We promise to the best of our power to prevent others from offending you and to bring as many as possible to follow you.

O loving Jesus, through the intercession of the Blessed Virgin Mother, our model in reparation, deign to receive the voluntary offering we make of this act of expiation; and by the crowning gift of perseverance keep us faithful unto death in our duty and the allegiance we owe to you, so that we may all one day come to that happy home, where with the Father and the Holy Spirit you live and reign, God, for ever and ever. Amen.

(A partial indulgence is granted to the faithful who piously recite the above act of reparation. A plenary indulgence is granted if it is publicly recited on the feast of the Most Sacred Heart of Jesus. See p59.)

A Novena for the First Fridays

The Novena (nine days of prayer) finds its origin in the nine days which passed between the Ascension and Pentecost, which the Apostles and Our Lady spent in constant prayer for the gift of the Holy Spirit. The Church has since approved of many 'novenas', including the following.

Novena Prayer

Sacred Heart of Jesus, I unite myself to your adoration, your burning love, your ardent zeal, you reparation, your thanksgiving, your firm confidence, your fervent prayers, your silence, your humility, your obedience, your gentleness and peace, your surpassing kindness, your universal charity, your deep recollection, your longing for the conversion of sinners, your union with your Heavenly Father, your intentions, desires, and will.

Love of the Heart of Jesus, inflame my heart; charity of the Heart of Jesus abound in my heart; strength of the Heart of Jesus uphold my heart; mercy of the Heart of Jesus forgive my heart; patience of the Heart of Jesus do not weary of my heart; kingdom of the heart of Jesus be established in my heart; wisdom of the Heart of Jesus teach my heart; will of the heart of Jesus dispose of my heart; zeal of the Heart of Jesus consume my heart. O Mary conceived without sin, pray for us to the Heart of Jesus.

Sweet Heart of Jesus who, through your tender love for the Church your Spouse, opened to her the riches and unspeakable sweetness of your Sacred heart, grant that our hearts may be enriched with the treasures it contains and replenished with its overflowing and unfailing delights.

Novena for the First Friday

Sacred Heart of Jesus, I unite myself:

To your adoration,
To your burning love,
To your ardent zeal,
To your reparation,
To your thanksgiving,
To your firm confidence,
To your fervent prayers,
To your silence,
To your humility,
To your obedience,
To your gentleness and peace,
To your surpassing kindness,
To your universal charity,
To your deep recollection,
To your intense desire for the conversion of sinners,
To your close union with the Heavenly Father,
To your intentions, desires, and will. Amen

Love of the Heart of Jesus,
Inflame my heart.
Charity of the Heart of Jesus,
Abound in my heart.
Strength of the Heart of Jesus,
Uphold my heart.
Mercy of the Heart of Jesus,

Forgive my heart.
Patience of the Heart of Jesus,
Do not weary of my heart.
Kingdom of the Heart of Jesus,
Be established in my heart.
Wisdom of the Heart of Jesus,
Teach my heart.
Will of the Heart of Jesus,
Dispose of my heart.
Zeal of the Hear of Jesus,
Consume my heart.
O Mary, conceived without sin,
Pray for us to the Heart of Jesus.

Sweet Jesus, who, through your tender love for the Church your Spouse, opened to her the riches and unspeakable sweetness of your Sacred Heart, grant that our hearts may be enriched with the treasures it contains and replenished with its overflowing and unfailing delights. Amen.

The devotion of the First Saturdays in honour of the Immaculate Heart of Mary

'The Heart of Mary is a sun that spreads its rays and its warmth throughout the world. It is constantly working in every possible way for the salvation of souls.'

(*St John Eudes*)

Devotion to Our Lady

As with devotion to the Sacred Heart of Jesus, devotion to Our Blessed Lady is as old as the Gospels themselves. She herself declared: 'All generations shall call me blessed' (*Lk* 1:48), and down the centuries this prophecy has been abundantly fulfiled. From the rough sketches we find on the walls of the catacombs, to the beautiful images of Mary in medieval art and literature, through the glories of the baroque pilgrimage churches of Europe and South America, and right down to the mass pilgrimages of today which honour Our Lady at shrines all over the world, the disciples of Jesus have always shown a trusting affection for his Virgin Mother. Undoubtedly this devotion to Mary is connected to her maternal heart. The tender care she showed for her divine Son, celebrated in the Gospels and in some of the greatest art of the western world, has inspired Christians to believe that they too can have some share in her love and protection. Moreover, the Gospels make it clear that Mary is not only the Mother of Jesus, but also his most faithful follower. This fidelity is based on her own prayerful reflection ('Mary treasured all these things and pondered them in her heart.' *Lk* 2:19), which keeps her always in Jesus' presence. She is privileged to witness the homage paid to him by the shepherds and the wise men at his birth (*Mt* 2:1ff), and later, it is under the care of Mary and Joseph that Jesus grows to maturity (*Lk* 2:40). She inspires the miracle which opens his public ministry (*Jn* 2:1ff), and is later present at the Crucifixion, when Jesus gives her to his beloved disciple, and to all his followers, with the words 'Behold your mother' (*Jn* 19:27). After the Resurrection, she continues faithful in prayer, and together with the Apostles experiences the outpouring of the Holy Spirit at Pentecost (*Ac* 1:14). Quiet, reflective, a woman who listens more than speaks, but capable of decisive action when the need arises, Mary is truly the model of a Christian life.

The Immaculate Heart

The Church has defined that Mary was entirely sinless, not only in the actions of her life but even from the moment of her conception. This was a special privilege granted her by God in order to prepare her to be the worthy Mother of his Son. This immaculate purity of Mary is precisely that which brings her close to us and fills her with pity for sinners, for whereas sin brings division, goodness and love bring union. From the Middle Ages onwards, many saints and spiritual writers began to focus on Mary's heart as the symbol of her closeness to God, and her sympathy for us. Among these great saints were St Anselm (+1109), St Bernard of Clairvaux (+1153) and St Bernadine of Sienna (+1444) who has been dubbed, 'The Doctor of the Heart of Mary'.

However, it was St John Eudes, who we have seen already as a great Apostle of the Sacred Heart, who also did most to establish devotion to the Immaculate Heart in the Church at large. From the Seventeenth Century onwards the devotion grew and strengthened, and was fostered again by the manifestation of the Miraculous Medal - which bears the symbols of both the Sacred Heart and Immaculate Heart - to St Catherine Labouré in 1830.

Our Lady's Saturday

Christians have honoured Mary in many different ways, one of which has been by devoting Saturday to Our Lady as her special day. This day was seen as especially appropriate since on the first Holy Saturday, when Jesus lay buried in the tomb, Mary was the only human being who retained her faith in him. The idea of dedicating Saturday to honour Our Lady is at least as old as Alcuin of York (+804), who mention sit in his writings, and continues to the present day - the Roman Missal provides a special Mass of the Blessed Virgin Mary to be used on Saturdays in Ordinary Time when no other feast is celebrated.

Since Saturday was considered Mary's special day, various observances arose connected to it. Often these devotions included the idea of reparation, since when we consider the perfect love of Mary's heart, we are filled with sorrow for our own sinfulness. For instance, during the seventeenth century the Dominican Order originated a devotion to Our Blessed Lady known as the 'Fifteen Saturdays. Those who wish to participate are asked to say five decades of the Rosary on each of the fifteen Saturdays that immediately precede the feast of Our Lady of the Rosary on October 7th, and to receive the Sacraments of Confession and Holy Communion. Among these Saturday devotions we should also mention the 'Saturday Communion of Reparation to Our Lady'. In 1898, Pope Leo XIII approved this observance, which was propagated by Sister Dolores Inglese (+1928) and the nuns of the Congregation of the Servants of Mary Reparatrix. On the first Saturday of every month, Holy Communion is received and an act of reparation made to compensate for any dishonour shown to Our Lady by the human race. This practice was further encouraged by Pope St Pius X.

However, the most famous and wide-spread of these Saturday devotions is undoubtedly the observance of the First Five Saturdays, which is intimately connected to the cult of the Immaculate Heart, and originates in the revelations made at Fatima in 1917.

Fatima

On 13th May 1917, Our Lady appeared to three shepherd-children, Lucia, Francisco and Jacinta, at the Cova da Iria near the town of Fatima in Portugal. She asked them to return on the thirteenth of every month leading up to October when she would tell them what she wished them to do. In the meantime she asked that the Rosary be recited daily and promised that she would give them a sign that would dispel any doubt they might have. During their subsequent visits to the Cova, Our Lady entrusted the children with prophetic warnings, asked that Russia be consecrated to her Immaculate Heart, and that a Holy Communion of reparation be made on the first Saturday of each month.

On 13th October, Our Lady identified herself as Our Lady of the Rosary, and fifty thousand people who had gathered at the Cova witnessed the "miracle of the sun dancing in the heavens." The children in ecstasy were also given visions of the Holy Family, Our Lady of Sorrows, and Our Lady of Mount Carmel. The legitimacy of the apparitions and the veneration of Our Lady of Fatima were approved in 1930. Between 1936 and 1942, Lucia made known further details of Our Lady's wishes: her pleas for the recitation of the Rosary, the practice of penance and sorrow for sin, and devotion to her Immaculate Heart. The Soviet Revolution in Russia, the rise of atheistic, totalitarian regimes across Europe and the outbreak of the Second World War increased interest in the circumstances of Fatima, and prompted the consecration of the world to the Immaculate Heart of Mary by Pope Pius XII in 1942. More recently, it is well-known that Pope John Paul II had a great devotion to Our

Lady of Fatima. On 13th May 1982, exactly a year after the unsuccessful attempt on his life, the Pope made a pilgrimage to Fatima to thank Our Lady for saving his life and, in his person, protecting the whole Church. At the square in front of the Basilica of Our Lady of Fatima, he renewed the consecration of the world to the Immaculate Heart of Mary.

The First Saturday Devotion

During her apparition at Fatima in July 1917, Our Lady said to Lucia, "I shall come to ask...that on the First Saturday of every month, Communions of reparation be made in atonement for the sins of the world." Although she made no further mention of this devotion at Fatima, on 10th December, 1925, our Blessed Mother again appeared to Lucia at Pentevedra, Spain, where the seer had been sent to the Dorothean Sisters to learn to read and write. It was there Our Lady completed her request for the Five First Saturdays and gave her great promise.

Appearing with the Queen of Heaven in that apparition was the Infant Jesus, who said to Lucia: "Have pity on the Heart of your Most Holy Mother. It is covered with thorns with which ungrateful men pierce it at every moment, and there is no one to remove them with an act of reparation." Our Lady then spoke: "See, my daughter, my Heart encircled by thorns with which ungrateful men pierce it at every moment by their blasphemies and ingratitude. Do you, at least, strive to console me. Tell them that I promise to assist at the hour of death with the graces necessary for salvation all those who, in order to make reparation to me, on the First Saturday of five successive months, go to confession, receive Holy Communion, say five decades of the Rosary, and keep me company for a quarter of an hour, meditating on the fifteen mysteries of the Rosary."

The elements of the devotion

The elements of this devotion, therefore, consist in the following:

1. **Sacramental Confession**;
2. **Holy Communion** received on five consecutive First Saturdays;
3. The recitation of **the Rosary** in addition to meditating on the mysteries for at least 15 minutes.

Since we have already spoken about Confession (see p13) and Holy Communion (see p19) when speaking of the First Friday Devotion (and everything said there is quite applicable to the First Saturday Devotion also), we shall concentrate here on the importance of praying the Rosary, and on what is meant by meditation upon its mysteries.

THE ROSARY

The Rosary is a vocal prayer said while reflecting upon the mysteries of Our Lord's life and passion in the company of Our Lady. It consists of a number of commonly-used prayers, which are counted with the assistance of a set of beads. While such 'prayer beads' are found in many religions, and have been used in Christianity from early times, the particular prayer known as 'The Rosary of the Blessed Virgin Mary', which was commended to the three children at Fatima, is particularly associated with St Dominic (+1221). Tradition has it that the saint received this rosary in an apparition of Our Lady, and used it with great success when preaching against the Albigensian heretics in France. From that time on, it has been one of the favourite prayers of the Church, used particularly in times of peril, and credited with winning many of the Church's victories over her foes.

How to pray the Rosary

Take a set of Rosary beads in your hand. Remember that every bead represents a prayer. Every 10 beads are called a DECADE. Each decade represents a MYSTERY - an event in the life of Jesus or Mary given to us to meditate on.

There are twenty mysteries of the Rosary, divided into four sets of five (the five mysteries known as 'The Luminous Mysteries' were devised by Pope John Paul II, and offered as an optional addition to the fifteen traditional mysteries in his Apostolic Letter *Rosarium Virginis Mariae*, of 2002). It is usual to pray only one set of mysteries at a time. These are the mysteries:

The Joyful Mysteries

1. The Annunciation
2. The Visitation
3. The Nativity of Jesus
4. The Presentation of Jesus
5. The Finding of the Child Jesus in the Temple

The Luminous Mysteries

1. The Baptism of Jesus
2. The Wedding at Cana
3. The Proclamation of the Kingdom
4. The Transfiguration
5. The Last Supper, & institution of the Eucharist

The Sorrowful Mysteries

1. The Agony in the Garden
2. The Scourging at the Pillar
3. The Crowning with thorns
4. The Carrying of the Cross
5. The Crucifixion

The Glorious Mysteries

1. The Resurrection
2. The Ascension
3. The Descent of the Holy Spirit at Pentecost
4. The Assumption of Mary into heaven
5. The Coronation of Mary as Queen of heaven and the glory of all the saints

To begin saying the Rosary:

1. Start by making the Sign of the Cross. Holding the crucifix at the end of the rosary, say the **Apostles Creed**:

I believe in God, the Father Almighty, creator of heaven and earth. I believe in Jesus Christ, his only Son, our Lord. He was conceived by Holy Spirit and born of the Virgin Mary. He suffered under Pontius Pilate, was crucified, died and was buried. He descended into hell. On the third day he rose again. He ascended into heaven and is seated at the right hand of the Father. He will come again to judge the living and the dead. I believe in the Holy Spirit, the Holy Catholic Church, the communion of saints, the forgiveness of sins, the resurrection of the body, and life everlasting. Amen.

2. On the 5 beads nearest to the crucifix say 5 prayers for the Pope's intentions - 1 *Our Father*, 3 *Hail Marys* and 1 *Glory be*.

3. You can now begin the first **decade** of the rosary. Before starting, picture the **mystery** you are about to meditate on (you will find further notes on meditation below). Say 1 *Our Father*, 10 *Hail Marys* and 1 *Glory be*, moving the beads through your fingers while you pray.

4. After the *Glory be*, it is appropriate to add the **Fatima Prayer**, taught by Our Lady to Lucia, Francisco and Jacinta:

O my Jesus, forgive us our sins, save us from the fires of hell, and lead all souls to heaven, especially those most in need of thy mercy.

5. Pray the next 5 decades in the same way as the first.

6. After the fifth decade, say the **Hail Holy Queen**:

Hail Holy Queen, Mother of mercy, hail our life our sweetness and our hope. To thee do we cry, poor banished children of Eve, to thee do we send up our sighs, mourning and weeping in this vale of tears. Turn then, most gracious advocate, thine eyes of mercy towards us, and after this our exile, show unto us the blessed fruit of thy womb Jesus. O clement, O loving, O sweet Virgin Mary.

Pray for us O holy Mother of God.

That we may be made worthy of the promises of Christ.

7. End by saying:

Let us pray. O God, whose only begotten Son, by his life, death and resurrection, has purchased for us the rewards of eternal life, grant, we beseech thee, that meditating upon these mysteries of the most holy rosary of the blessed Virgin Mary, we may both imitate what they contain, and obtain what they promise, through the same Christ our Lord. Amen.

May the divine assistance remain always with us. May the souls of the faithful departed, through the mercy of God, rest in peace. Amen.

'MEDITATING ON THE MYSTERIES'

The notes above explain the 'mechanics' of how to recite the Rosary. However, Our Lady at Fatima explicitly asked that this prayer be said while meditating on the mysteries for at least 15 minutes. This is one of the required elements of the First Saturday devotion.

In fact, it would be quite difficult to recite 5 decades of the Rosary in less than 15 minutes, and if we did so it would almost certainly be a sign that we were not offering this prayer with sufficient care and attention. As we noted before, in the context of the First Fridays, attempting to fulfil the requirements of these devotions in a superstitious or minimalist way is quite contrary to the mind of the Church, and would not bring the blessings promised. In this, as in every element of the Christian life, generosity and a willing heart are essential.

Once we have understood this, then Our Lady's request that we meditate while praying the Rosary will not seem difficult at all. Indeed, it simply requires that we *recite* the prayers at a reasonable pace, and that while we are doing so we *think* about the mystery we are praying. We should remember that the words, in this instance, are not important - they simply form a backdrop against which we contemplate the most significant events in the lives of Jesus and Mary.

The way we choose to meditate will vary from person to person. Some people will find it useful to imagine the scene they contemplating in considerable detail. For instance, suppose we are praying the First Joyful Mystery, the Annunciation. Some people will like to picture the whole scene - they will see the Angel Gabriel appearing to Mary, and will imagine what Mary looks like, her general appearance and her attitude of recollection. Then they will look within, at her thoughts, her faith, her affections. By contemplating the mystery in this way, they may perhaps be able to imitate Mary's virtues in their own lives.

For other people, however, imagining the scene in this sort of detail would be unhelpful, and a distraction from prayer. All they need is some simple idea to focus their minds. The great spiritual writer, Dom John Chapman, once advised one of his correspondents:

'I should not worry *how* to say the Rosary. The easiest thing is to have some *simple* thought in connection with each mystery; e.g. the first mystery: that Our Lady simply gives herself up to God; or the last mystery: just Heaven; and so forth.' *(The Spiritual Letters of Dom John Chapman OSB*.)

We must each work out for ourselves which way of meditation is best for us. The most important thing is to realise that meditation is not difficult! As a wise and holy English bishop once wrote:

'The great business of mental prayer is *thinking* and *loving*: and who is there that can even live without *thinking* and *loving*?' (Bishop Richard Challoner, *Meditations for every Day of the Year*.)

OTHER PRAYERS TO OUR LADY

Just as the First Friday devotion presupposes that all those who practice it will grow in fervour towards the Sacred Heart, so it is hoped that all those who observe the Five First Saturdays will grow in love for Our Lady. There are many ways we can express this love, for example, in celebrating the Feast of the Immaculate Heart of Mary (which in the Ordinary Form of the Roman Missal is kept on the day following the Feast of the

Sacred Heart). It may also be helpful to make use of these other prayers in honour of Mary, which although not part of the First Saturday devotion as such, certainly lead us closer to the Immaculate Heart of the Mother of God.

The Litany of the Loreto

Lord have mercy.
Lord have mercy.
Christ have mercy.
Christ have mercy.
Lord have mercy.
Lord have mercy.
Christ hear us.
Christ graciously hear us.
God the Father of heaven,
have mercy on us.
God the Son, Redeemer
of the world,
have mercy on us.
God the Holy Spirit,
have mercy on us.
Holy Trinity, one God,
have mercy on us.
Holy Mary,
pray for us. (repeat hereafter)
Holy Mother of God,

Holy Virgin of virgins,
Mother of Christ,
Mother of divine grace,
Mother most pure,
Mother most chaste,
Mother inviolate,
Mother undefiled,
Mother most lovable,
Mother most admirable,
Mother of good counsel,
Mother of our Creator,
Mother of our Saviour,
Virgin most prudent,
Virgin most venerable,
Virgin most renowned,
Virgin most powerful,
Virgin most merciful,
Virgin most faithful,
Mirror of Justice,
Seat of wisdom,

Cause of our joy,
Spiritual vessel,
Vessel of honour,
Singular vessel of devotion,
Mystical rose,
Tower of David,
Tower of ivory,
House of gold,
Ark of the covenant,
Gate of heaven,
Morning Star,
Health of the sick,
Refuge of sinners,
Comfort of the afflicted,
Help of Christians,

Queen of Angels,
Queen of Patriarchs,
Queen of Prophets,
Queen of Apostles
Queen of Martyrs,
Queen of Confessors,
Queen of Virgins,
Queen of all Saints,
Queen conceived
without original sin,
Queen assumed into heaven,
Queen of the most
holy Rosary,
Queen of the Family,
Queen of Peace.

Lamb of God, you take away the sins of the world,
spare us, O Lord.
Lamb of God, you take away the sins of the world,
graciously hear us, O Lord.
Lamb of God, you take away the sins of the world,
have mercy on us.
V. Pray for us, O holy Mother of God.
R. *That we may be made worthy of the promises of Christ.*

Let us pray:
Lord God, give to your people the joy of continual health
in mind and body.
With the prayers of the Virgin Mary to help us,
guide us through the sorrows of this life to eternal happiness
in the life to come.
Grant this through our Lord Jesus Christ, your Son,
who lives and reigns with you and the Holy Spirit,
one God, for ever and ever. R. Amen.

The Memorare

Remember, O most gracious Virgin Mary,
that never was it known that anyone
who fled to thy protection, implored thy help,
or sought thy intercession, was left unaided.
Inspired by this confidence I fly unto thee,
O Virgin of virgins, my Mother.
To thee do I come, before thee I stand, sinful and sorrowful.
O Mother of the Word Incarnate, despise not my petitions,
but in thy mercy hear and answer me. Amen.

We Fly to Thy Protection - Sub Tuum Praesidium

We fly to thy protection,
O holy Mother of God,
despise not our petitions in our necessities,
but deliver us always from all dangers,
O glorious and blessed Virgin.

Prayer for England

O Blessed Virgin Mary, Mother of God,
and our most gentle queen and mother,
look down in mercy upon England, your dowry,
and upon us all who greatly hope and trust in you.
By you it was that Jesus, our Saviour and our hope,
was given to the world;
and he has given you to us that we may hope still more.

Plead for us your children,
whom you received and accepted at the foot of the cross,
O mother of sorrows.
Pray for our separated brethren,
that in the one true fold of Christ,
we may all be united under the care of Pope N.,
the chief shepherd of Christ's flock.
Pray for us all, dear mother,
that by faith, and fruitful in good works,
we may all deserve to see and praise God,
together with you in our heavenly home.

The Morning Offering

O Jesus, through the most pure heart of Mary,
I offer you all the prayers, works and sufferings of this day
for all the intentions of your divine Heart.
O most Sacred Heart of Jesus,
I place all my trust in Thee (*three times*). Amen.

The Four Marian Antiphons

These four antiphons in honour of Our Lady from part of the Divine Office, or 'Prayer of the Church', and may be used at Compline ('Night prayer'). Traditionally different antiphons are used at different seasons of the year, as noted, but in our private prayers we may, of course, make use of them at any time or season.

Alma Redemptoris Mater

(From the First Sunday of Advent until Candlemas, 2nd February)

Alma Redemptoris Mater, quae pervia caeli
Porta manes, et stella maris, succurre cadenti,
Surgere qui curat, populo: tu quae genuisti,
Natura mirante, tuum sanctum Genitorem
Virgo prius ac posterius, Gabrielis ab ore
Sumens illud Ave, peccatorum miserere.

(Translation)

Mother of Christ, hear thou thy people's cry
Star of the deep and Portal of the sky!
Mother of Him who thee made from nothing made.
Sinking we strive and call to thee for aid:
Oh, by what joy which Gabriel brought to thee,
Thou Virgin first and last, let us thy mercy see.

Ave, Regina caelorum

(From 3rd February until Eastertide)
Ave, Regina caelorum,
Ave, Domina Angelorum:
Salve, radix, salve, porta,
Ex qua mundo lux est orta:
Gaude, Virgo gloriosa,
Super omnes speciosa,
Vale, o valde decora,
Et pro nobis Christum exora.

(Translation)
Hail, O Queen of Heav'n enthron'd,
Hail, by angels Mistress own'd
Root of Jesse, Gate of morn,
Whence the world's true light was born.
Glorious Virgin, joy to thee,
Lovliest whom in Heaven they see,
Fairest thou where all are fair!
Plead with Christ our sins to spare.

Regina caeli

(During Eastertide)
Regina, caeli, laetare, alleluia:
Quia quem meruisti portare, alleluia,
Resurrexit sicut dixit, alleluia.
Ora pro nobis Deum, alleluia.

(Translation)

O Queen of heaven rejoice! alleluia:
For He whom thou didst merit to bear, alleluia,
Hath arisen as he said, alleluia.
Pray for us to God, alleluia.

Salve Regina

(From the end of Eastertide until the beginning of Advent)
Salve, Regina, mater misericordiae, vita, dulcedo, et spes
nostra, salve. Ad te clamamus exsules filii Hevae. Ad te
suspiramus, gementes et flentes in hac lacrimarum valle.
Eia, ergo, advocata nostra, illos tuos misericordes oculos
ad nos converte. Et Iesum, benedictum fructum ventris
tui, nobis post hoc exsilium ostende.
O clemens, O pia, O dulcis Virgo Maria. Amen.

(Translation)

Hail holy Queen, Mother of mercy, our life, our
sweetness, and our hope. To thee do we cry, poor banished
children of Eve. To thee do we send up our sighs,
mourning and weeping in this vale of tears. Turn then,
most gracious Advocate, thine eyes of mercy toward us.
And after this our exile show unto us the blessed fruit of
thy womb, Jesus.
O clement, O loving, O sweet Virgin Mary. Amen.

A NOTE ON INDULGENCES

Some of the prayers and devotional practices set out in this booklet attract what is known as an 'indulgence' (for instance, those who make the 'Holy Hour' in the presence of the Blessed Sacrament may obtain a plenary indulgence for doing so). The following is a brief statement of the doctrine of indulgences:

'Indulgences are the remission before God of the temporal punishment due to sins whose guilt has already been forgiven. The faithful Christian who is duly disposed gains the indulgence under prescribed conditions for either himself or the departed. Indulgences are granted through the ministry of the Church which, as the dispenser of the grace of redemption, distributes the treasury of merits of Christ and the Saints' *CCC*, 312

Any Catholic in a state of grace can gain an indulgence. To gain an indulgence we must have the intention of doing so, and we must say certain prayers, or carry out certain good works to which the Church has specifically attached an indulgence.

Indulgences can be either 'partial' or 'plenary'. A partial indulgence remits part of the temporal punishment due to our sins - a 'plenary' indulgence omits the *whole* of that punishment: it is a great gift of grace which prepares us to meet God immediately. For this reason certain conditions are attached to obtaining of a plenary indulgence. These conditions are: going to Confession, receiving Holy Communion and praying for the Pope's intentions. We should try to receive Holy Communion on the same day that we gain the indulgence - we are allowed to go to Confession either a few days before or a few days afterwards. The prayers for the Pope do not need to be lengthy - an *Our Father*, *Hail Mary* and *Glory be* are usual. Finally, to gain a plenary indulgence a person needs to be free 'from all attachment to sin'. Without such detachment only a partial indulgence will be gained.

A Simple Rosary Book

Enriched by the history, customs and scripture that surround the Holy Rosary, many today are rediscovering this prayer which lies at the heart of Catholic spirituality. Through 'this school of prayer' (St John Paul II) disciples grow in love for Christ through Mary, mother of the Lord.

Designed for those familiar with the prayer as well as for newcomers, this text clearly explains how to pray the Rosary. Prayers and Scripture passages associated with the Rosary are also included.

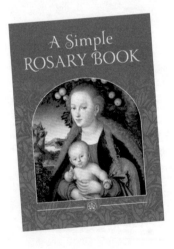

ISBN: 978 1 86082 925 3

CTS Code: D776

A Simple Penance Book

Pope Francis says "God never tires of forgiving us; we are the ones who tire of seeking his mercy". The practice of Confession, Penance and Reconciliation bears rich fruit not only in the Christian's own life but impacts directly on the lives of those around us.

The true joy needed in the mission to share our faith arises from a real experience that our sins have been forgiven. How to prepare and celebrate the sacrament is explained both for newcomers and the already familiar.

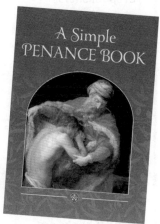

ISBN: 978 1 86082 926 0

CTS Code: D777